THE KEYS CREED:
88 KEYS

THE KEYS CREED:
88 KEYS

JAY KEYS

2019

Copyright © 2019 by Jay Keys

All rights reserved. This book or any portion thereof may not be reproduced or used in any manner whatsoever without the express written permission of the publisher except for the use of brief quotations in a book review or scholarly journal.

First Printing: 2019

ISBN **978-0-578-56451-7**

www.thewinproject.net

Dedication

The Keys Creed is dedicated to my children and their children's children, on to the generations to come.

"As for me and my house, we will serve the Lord."

Psalm 103:17-18
But from everlasting to everlasting the Lord's love is with those who fear him, and his righteousness with their children's children... with those who keep his covenant and remember to obey his precepts. Amen!

Sincerely yours,

James Clark Keys (Jay)

Preface

It is said that when you come into the understanding of who you are the restraints of life are forced to set you free. I carried the question of "who am I" most of my life. I knew my name and the physical persona I carried with me by way of my flesh, but as I got older, I began to figure out that was not enough. Something was missing. The trials of life brought too many inconsistencies, depression, anxiety, frustration, suicidal thoughts, perversion, lust... Not only did I carry the question of "who am I," most of my life, I also carry the name of a man whom I have never met and in my mid-twenties I began to question "who was he." My name belonged to my Grandfather and in 1977 my Mother became pregnant. I was the second of her four children and, as life would be beginning for me another life would come to a tragic end. My Grandfather passed away four months into my Mother's pregnancy of a massive heart attack at the age of forty-nine. He died on May the seventh of 1977 and eight months later I came into the world on January 7th, 1978. My parents named me James Clark Keys but, most of my life I identified with the name Jay. I assume this was the nickname of which my parents chose to create some distinction from my Mother's father, James Clark. From what I understand, he was an honorable man, well respected and big in stature (6ft. 8inches). I recall my grandmother saying, "ain't nobody like James Clark", which was her reason for never dating nor looking to remarry ever again. She passed almost 40 years later in February of 2015 as a proud widow; how phenomenal of a woman was she!

My childhood was full. I was naturally gifted; I experienced a lot of attention and success. I decided to attend Bowling Green St. University on a basketball scholarship and pursue my dream of becoming a professional athlete. It didn't matter to me be it the NBA or overseas I had one occupation in mind, and it was to get paychecks playing basketball. As I now know all the things that we are in pursuit of will show up in the form of a test and my test happened to be my coach. He was a player and an assistant under the Indiana University program for 14yrs and carried the same spirit with him that he shared with his mentor. He was the first person to ever strip something from me that brought me complete joy and from that point on I was introduced to the spirit of depression. I eventually transferred schools, but my life and my relationship with basketball were never the same. I quickly became codependent on marijuana and alcohol. They were the release and crutch that I chose to stand in life. I had multiple women and no direction unable to trust or commit to anything or anyone. This mentality carried on from my twenties into my thirties until God began to have His way.

One day when I was driving on my way home from work, I was in deep thought about my Grandfather, his name, his attachment, and his association to me. I questioned, "why do I carry his name, who is he, what was he like, what were his thoughts, how did he walk and talk...?" Then, I began to think about my kids and my kids, kids and what could I leave behind if they ever shared the same thoughts regarding me. How can I help them navigate through life when confusion tries to step in? So, I decided to write some thoughts, some principles to leave behind in the form of good counsel and that way I would never leave them and at the same time provide some insight into who I am and what I stand for. Funny thing was, I still didn't know myself but as I began to write, research, stumble across scripture and information little did I know that I was on my journey towards truth. I always had a foundation in Christ, but I never tried to learn who He is for myself, nor apply any of His principles towards my life. It took three years to put this project together from 2016 to 2019, and now here we are, The Keys Creed, 88 Keys.

Why 88 Keys? Of course, it started as a play on words because of my last name and the melodic keys of a piano. I wanted my words of wisdom to be exactly that for my children translating into a rhythmic melody that would guide them throughout life. Then, it became that much more significant when I found out the importance of keys and its translation as law, to gain access to or understanding of, the ability to lock or unlock. At this point I am intrigued, I had to find out what the translation of the number 88 is. "A powerful vibration telling of achievements, success, striving forward, progress and attainment. Angel **Number 88** is a message that you are to keep your finances in check to ensure that you have set aside solid foundations for yourself and your loved ones. This will ensure your future prosperity." In essence, this book is designed by law to lock and unlock achievements, success, progress, and attainment. Keeping finances in check to ensure a solid foundation for yourself and your loved ones. Wow!!! I couldn't have made that up if I wanted to. I didn't say it, it was already written, my job was to be obedient.

I thank God for the understanding and revelation of obedience and because of it I have found my truth. My childhood best friend died in January of 2019 and it changed my life forever. It was the first time I ever had to deal with someone close to me my age leaving this earth by way of natural causes. I remember when we were 11 years old and I had asked him if he ever accepted Christ. He said, no. He was one of the first I had ever witnessed and prayed with seeking Christ to come into his heart. Our bond was sealed in a way that extended beyond what we see in the physical, at that moment it became eternal. On the day of his funeral, I experienced something beyond explanation. My mother grabbed me by the arm and walked me to the casket because she knew my disturbance of attending funerals. I had no intention of saying goodbye like that but what was meant for me took place at that moment. As I viewed the body I was overwhelmed with emotion and it appeared as if my spirit had left my physical space. It only lasted for a moment, but I was able to look down on everyone in the sanctuary including myself as I stood frozen in front of the corpse. I returned to myself and I heard a voice say, "but for the grace of God this could be you." I believe at that moment my spirit connected with the Spirit of Truth and by way of the Holy Spirit, I became new.

My desire for you as you read this collection of principals is that you will focus on one thought per day. Take the time to truly digest and reflect. Allow what you are reading to minister to your entire being, spiritual, mental and emotional, and then apply it. I believe that you will be surprised by the things you learn about yourself. Be blessed!

THE KEYS CREED: 88 KEYS

1. Deposit positive content into your being and it will add value to your soul. The soul is the central processing unit comprised of the mind, will, and emotion.

   Spiritual Content: Proverbs 23:7
   For as he thinks in his heart, so is he. "Eat and drink!" He says to you, but his heart is not with you.

   Natural Content: Our experiences cause us to choose, think and act upon our circumstances concerning relationships with others.

   Key Question: What are you consuming that influences your mind, will, and emotion?

   Key Terms: content, value, soul, central processing unit, mind, will, emotion

   Key Take-Away for Today:

2. The law of attraction begins with a thought that activates the unseen through vibrations of energy-producing life. Be wise as to what you consume, think and speak.

Spiritual Content: Matthew 21:22
And all things, whatsoever ye shall ask in prayer, believing, ye shall receive.

Natural Content: Be careful as to what you think and say because those very thoughts and words potentially will manifest in physical nature.

Key Question: What type of influences are your thoughts causing to be attracted to you?

Keys Terms: law of attraction, activate, vibration, energy

Key Take-Away for Today:

3. The world has been constructed upon manipulation and facades. People want honesty but won't adhere to the truth. The truth will always force people to relinquish control.

Spiritual Content: John 8:32
And ye shall know the truth, and the truth shall make you free.

Natural Content: This speaks to the gatekeepers that hold the keys to social and economic justice but, withhold the truth from the people to control the masses.

Key Question: Is it significant to live in truth? Why?

Key Terms: constructed, manipulation, facade, honesty, adhere, truth, relinquish, control

Key Take-Away for Today:

4. I see the beauty in my upbringing valued on righteousness because I have experienced living outside of principle.

Spiritual Content: 1 John 3:7
Little children, let no man deceive you: he that doeth righteousness is righteous, even as he is righteous.

Natural Content: A foundation based on biblical principles will always speak to the integrity and character of self.

Key Question: Why are principles fundamental to obtaining righteousness?

Key Terms: beauty, upbringing, value, righteousness

Key Take-Away for Today:

5. The power of thought is in direct correlation to the company you keep.

   Spiritual Content: Proverbs 13:20
   He that walketh with wise men shall be wise: but a companion of fools shall be destroyed.

   Natural Content: There is a saying, "Show me your five closest friends and I will show you your future."

   Key Question: Do you think and act like those you spend time with the most?

   Key Terms: power, thought, correlation, company

   Key Take-Away for Today:

6. My children are my world. They help define my being, and my daughter is the vital organ. She will forever remain my heart.

Spiritual Content: Exodus 20:12
Honour thy father and thy mother: that thy days may be long upon the land which the Lord thy God giveth thee.

Natural Content: Motivation comes from the things that we cherish the most. I hope that I will leave a great legacy for generations to come.

Key Question: What motivates you?

Key Terms: define, being, vital, organ, remain

Key Take-Away for Today:

7. The preservation of your legacy will begin once you identify who you are and, remaining true to integrity.

Spiritual Content: Proverbs 20:7
The just man walketh in his integrity, his children are blessed after him.

Natural Content: Not many can say that they are in public who they are at home.

Key Question: How do you want to be remembered?

Key Terms: legacy, parallel, integrity

Key Take-Away for Today:

8. Your goals will be counterproductive if you are not intentional about your dreams. Activate the spirit of truth and you will find your treasure.

Spiritual Content: Acts 2:17
And it shall come to pass in the last days, saith God, I will pour out of my Spirit upon all flesh: and your sons and your daughters shall prophesy, and your young men shall see visions, and your old men shall dream dreams."

Natural Content: Never give up on your dreams because it was embedded in your DNA as a birthright for the Kingdom's glory.

Key Question: What are you achieving short term and long term in your process of becoming?

Key Terms: goals, counterproductive, intentional, dreams, activate, spirit, truth, treasure

Key Take-Away for Today:

9. Life is a vapor and our memories are the only thing that will remain with us after death.

Spiritual Content: Proverbs 10:7
The memory of the just is blessed: but the name of the wicked shall rot.

Natural Content: Make the most of every moment and be at peace with God because the soul is the only thing that will transfer over to the afterworld.

Key Question: How important is God's view of your life?

Key Terms: vapor, memories, remain, death

Key Take-Away for Today:

10. The presence of the Lord is an unspeakable joy. You will find fulfillment, pleasure, and peace in it on earth.

Spiritual Content: Psalms 16:11
Thou wilt shew me the path of life: in thy presence is fullness of joy; at thy right hand, there are pleasures forevermore.

Natural Content: In our life experiences we will have trials and tribulations, but we can also experience thy will be done on earth as it is in heaven if we are obedient to God's statutes and laws.

Key Question: Are you seeking God's presence?

Key Terms: presence, Lord, joy, fulfillment, pleasure, peace

Key Take-Away for Today:

11. It's not about what they're doing as opposed to what you are doing. Accountability of self is your line of credit. Protect your name so that it may go well before you amongst others.

Spiritual Content: Luke 16:10-12
He that is faithful in that which is least is faithful also in much: and he that is unjust in the least is unjust also in much. If therefore ye have not been faithful in the unrighteous mammon, who will commit to your trust the true riches? And if ye have not been faithful in that which is another man's, who shall give you that which is your own.

Natural Content: Be your own man no matter the circumstance. Never compromise who you are for personal gain. Your integrity will surface by the testing of your character.

Key Question: Why is accountability to yourself important?

Key Terms: oppose, accountability, self, credit, protect, well, amongst

Key Take-Away for Today:

12. I believe we are all created equal up until our first breath.

Spiritual Content: 1 Samuel 16:7
But the Lord said unto Samuel, Look not on his countenance, or on the height of his stature; because I have refused him: for the Lord seeth not as man seeth; for man looketh on the outward appearance, but the Lord looketh on the heart.

Natural Content: Society will pass judgment based on your skin, gender, beliefs, education, appearance... but, it is the heart of "Man" that should be judged alone.

Key Question: How do you handle inequality towards yourself and others?

Key Terms: believe, created, equal

Key Take-Away for Today:

13. The demise of man will always be based upon sin and the ability to control our free will, CHOICES!

Spiritual Content: James 1:13, 14
Let no man say when he is tempted, I am tempted of God: for God cannot be tempted with evil, neither tempteth he any man: But every man is tempted, when he is drawn away of his own lust, and enticed.

Natural Content: We have witnessed time and time again those who have lost all possessions be it material and/or relational based on a poor choice. See clearly as to what awaits you on the other side of the fence.

Key Question: Are your choices developing you as a better person?

Key Terms: demise, man, sin, ability, control, free, will, choices

Key Take-Away for Today:

14. When you support other people's visions your dreams will manifest itself into reality.

Spiritual Content: Luke 6:38
Give, and it shall be given unto you; good measure, pressed down, and shaken together, and running over, shall men give into your bosom. For with the same measure that ye mete withal it shall be measured to you again.

Natural Content: Be of good service by investing in something that does not belong to you. The reward will return through God's favor upon your life.

Key Question: What are you doing to support others?

Key Terms: support, visions, dreams, manifest, reality

Key Take-Away for Today:

15. Life is the toughest opponent you will ever face. There is no preparation but there is a blueprint, the B-I-B-L-E. Basic Instructions Before Leaving Earth.

Spiritual Content: John 3:16
For God so loved the world that he gave his only begotten son that who so ever would believeth in him should not perish but have everlasting life.

Natural Content: When dealing with life's challenges seek consultation from the constitution of life. God provided us with the greatest gift, his son Jesus Christ, who restored us by way of death and resurrection. His example of how to live has freed us from all captivity.

Key Question: Do you know who Christ is?

Key Terms: life, toughest, opponent, preparation, blueprint, Bible

Key Take-Away for Today:

16. Remain honest and humble to the people in your life that are willing to go the extra mile for you. Not everyone is genuine.

Spiritual Content: Proverbs 12:26
The godly give good advice to their friends; the wicked lead them astray.

Natural Content: Not everyone is a friend. Some get close only to destroy you. Pay attention to who comes in your life. Test the spirit by the spirit and you will know who who is.

Key Question: How much value do you place on others?

Key Terms: remain, honest, humble, willing, extra, genuine

Key Take-Away for Today:

17. Momentum is everything. When you peak at the right time and the chemistry is there you usually have the pedigree of a champion.

Spiritual Content: Philippians 3:14
I press toward the mark for the prize of the high calling of God in Christ Jesus.

Natural Content: Good chemistry will always create an atmosphere for success. I advise, stand clear of toxic behavior. Those with toxic behavior have no regard for your well-being.

Key Question: Why would poor chemistry negatively impact your outcome?

Key Term: momentum, everything, peak, chemistry, usually, pedigree, champion

Key Take-Away for Today:

18. I applaud those that made it, even more, I salute those who remained grounded, and opened doors of opportunity for others.

Spiritual Content: 1 John 3:17
But whoso hath this world's good, and seeth his brother have need, and shutteth up his bowels of compassion from him, how dwelleth the love of God in him?

Natural Content: Those who are in a position to pull up the next individual that has proved worthy of qualification should not turn a blind eye. That person who needed a hand could be the difference in a multitude of lives.

Key Question: Why is it important to help others when you are in a position to do so?

Key Terms: applaud, salute, remained, grounded, opportunity

Key Take-Away for Today:

19. To be of service to others start with compassion.

Spiritual Content: Matthew 9:36-38
When he saw the crowds, he had compassion on them, because they were harassed and helpless, like sheep without a shepherd. Then he said to his disciples, "The harvest is plentiful but the workers are few. Ask the Lord of the harvest, therefore, to send out workers into his harvest field."

Natural Content: You could be all the difference in the world for someone by simply showing them you care. Emotional discourse and suffering usually stem from rejection.

Key Question: Why is compassion necessary?

Key Terms: service, start, compassion

Key Take-Away for Today:

20. A wise man is a sound listener.

Spiritual Content: Proverbs 19:20
Hear counsel, and receive instruction, that thou mayest be wise in thy latter end.

Natural Content: There is a saying that, you have two ears and one mouth for a reason. Be quick to listen and slow to speak. Knowledge has always been passed by way of someone else's experience.

Key Question: Are you willing to be a good listener and apply wisdom to your life?

Key Terms: wise, sound, listener

Key Take-Away for Today:

21. A merciful man is charitable, and his benevolence will bring prosperity.

Spiritual Content: Deuteronomy 15:7-11

If anyone is poor among your fellow Israelites in any of the towns of the land the Lord your God is giving you, do not be hardhearted or tightfisted toward them. Rather, be openhanded and freely lend them whatever they need. Be careful not to harbor this wicked thought: "The seventh year, the year for canceling debts, is near," so that you do not show ill will toward the needy among your fellow Israelites and give them nothing. They may then appeal to the Lord against you, and you will be found guilty of sin. Give generously to them and do so without a grudging heart; then because of this, the Lord your God will bless you in all your work and in everything you put your hand to. There will always be poor people in the land. Therefore, I command you to be openhanded toward your fellow Israelites who are poor and needy in your land.

Natural Content: The unselfish man will never go without and the more we give the more we shall receive.

Key Question: What type of selfless acts have you displayed?

Key Terms: merciful, charitable, benevolence, prosperity

Key Take-Away for Today:

22. Every man is entitled to respect, but their actions will determine the level of it.

Spiritual Content: 1 Peter 2:17
Show proper respect to everyone, love the family of believers, fear God, honor the emperor.

Natural Content: Feed people with a long-handled spoon. Meaning, you should respect everyone you come in contact with, but the degree of respect must be earned.

Key Question: How often are you considerate towards others?

Key Terms: entitled, respect, actions, determine, level

Key Take-Away for Today:

23. Your attitude will always affect your inspiration and destination. The key is how you honestly view your attitude to be.

Spiritual Content: Ephesians 4:31-32
Get rid of all bitterness, rage, and anger, brawling and slander, along with every form of malice. Be kind and compassionate to one another, forgiving each other, just as in Christ God forgave you.

Natural Content: If you see yourself with a good attitude you will conform yourself as such; transforming all circumstances into a positive outlook.

Key Question: Does your attitude impact relationships negatively or positively?

Key Terms: attitude, affect, inspiration, destination, key, honestly, view

Key Take-Away for Today:

24. Faith is always the calm when you are in a storm. Wait on God and allow Him to convict your heart and He will show Himself in a mighty way.

Spiritual Content: Ezra 10:1
Now while Ezra was praying and making confession, weeping and prostrating himself before the house of God, a very large assembly, men, women and children, gathered to him from Israel; for the people wept bitterly.

Natural Content: It takes faith to calm waters, but conviction will move mountains.

Key Question: How relevant is your faith in regards to difficult circumstances?

Key Terms: faith, calm, storm, convict, mighty

Key Take-Away for Today:

25. Sometimes, when life is like a foreign language, seek a mentor for interpretation.

Spiritual Content: Proverbs 9:9
Give instruction to a wise man, and he will be yet wiser: teach a just man, and he will increase in learning. Because of life's uncertainties, the opinions of those that have obtained success are extremely valuable.

Natural Content: Understand that the most successful people in life did not become successful on their own. At some point, they were nurtured and counseled by someone along the way.

Key Question: Who is your mentor?

Key Terms: foreign, mentor, interpretation

Key Take-Away for Today:

26. Be a Victor and not a Vic-DUMB!

Spiritual Content: 1 Corinthians 15:57
But thanks [be] to God, which giveth us the victory through our Lord Jesus Christ.

Natural Content: Declare your victory over all things. For it is already finished. To think otherwise concerning all things challenges the truth.

Key Question: Are you hindering yourself because of a victim mentality?

Key Terms: victor, victim

Key Take-Away for Today:

27. To have peace one must become secure with self.

Spiritual Content: Joshua 1:9
Have not I commanded thee? Be strong and of good courage; be not afraid, neither be thou dismayed: for the LORD thy God [is] with thee whithersoever thou goest.

Natural Content: To know self is to know God and to know God is to know the truth. Providing a SHALOM type of peace within you.

Key Question: What causes you to feel insecure? And why?

Key Terms: peace, secure, self

Key Take-Away for Today:

28. Renew your mind every day, because seasons change, and I AM constantly moving.

Spiritual Content: 2 Corinthians 4:16
For which cause we faint not; but though our outward man perish, yet the inward [man] is renewed day by day.

Natural Content: As the body of Christ we must know how and when God is moving so we can remain in the flow of the spirit. Do not miss out on your blessing.

Key Question: Why is it important to begin every day with a fresh mindset?

Key Terms: renew, mind, seasons, I AM, constantly

Key Take-Away for Today:

29. A kind word can change an atmosphere.

Spiritual Content: Proverbs 15:1
A soft answer turneth away wrath: but grievous words stir up anger.

Natural Content: Our words have the power that can free or enslave the mind. The use of our words can uplift or destroy people, places and things.

Key Question: How do you feel when someone is polite to you?

Key Terms: kind, atmosphere

Key Take-Away for Today:

30. As a reflection, the way you are living will always reveal you. No matter the façade portrayed in public the truth will always surface.

Spiritual Content: 2 Timothy 2:15
Do your best to present yourself to God as one approved, a worker who has no need to be ashamed, rightly handling the word of truth.

Natural Content: We all have skeletons, and, no matter the cost be sure to stand on truth.

Key Question: How can you justify a lie worth living?

Key Terms: reflection, living, reveal, façade, portrayed, public, surface

Key Take-Away for Today:

31. Identify your passion because the ability that you are given along with consistency and diligence can become the pathway to success.

Spiritual Content: Colossians 3:23
And whatsoever ye do, do it heartily, as to the Lord, and not unto men;

Natural Content: Stick with the abilities you are gifted with and enjoy the process of perfection. It is on this journey that you will find success.

Key Question: What do you enjoy doing that does not feel like a burden of work?

Key Terms: identify, passion, ability, consistency, diligence, pathway, success

Key Take-Away for Today:

32. Love yourself, and it will become therapeutic compensation for the voids that are currently in your life.

Spiritual Content: Proverbs 19:8
He that getteth wisdom loveth his own soul: he that keepeth understanding shall find good.

Natural Content: Self - love is the most honest love you could give. It frees you from the deception of hate. Truth is in love, and love begins in truth.

Key Question: How often do you reassure yourself that you are loved?

Key Terms: love, therapeutic, compensation, voids

Key Take-Away for Today:

33. Confidence is everything! Set high expectations because what you don't achieve you will gain wisdom along the way.

Spiritual Content: Philippians 1:6
Being confident of this very thing, that he which hath begun a good work in you will perform [it] until the day of Jesus Christ:

Natural Content: In pursuit of accomplishment there will be mistakes along the way, but how we go about changing them exhibits growth. Failures should never be viewed as losses; they are simply learning experiences.

Key Question: What are some abilities you feel confident and not so confident in?

Key Terms: confidence, expectations, achieve, wisdom

Key Take-Away for Today:

34. Good humanity will continue to decline if we value social media more than physical communication, discipline, and structure.

Spiritual Content: Galatians 6:2
Bear ye one another's burdens, and so fulfill the law of Christ.

Natural Content: Social media has created more social lines of communication while causing relational beings to be less personable, hardening our innate senses towards social behavior. We are becoming uncomfortable verbally and socially awkward.

Key Question: Are you spending more time on your electronic device communicating than you are with the people in your own home?

Key Terms: humanity, decline, social media, physical, communication, discipline, structure

Key Take-Away for Today:

35. In this world, standing for what is right will be scrutinized, disagreed upon or simply disregarded due to the forces of darkness.

Spiritual Content: Ephesians 6:12
For we wrestle not against flesh and blood, but against principalities, against powers, against the rulers of the darkness of this world, against spiritual wickedness in high [places].

Natural Content: When principles and values shift to political correctness as opposed to truth, the core of the issue is beyond what we see on the surface. Pay attention to those who lobby for the positions of "gatekeeper" they are usually placed to uphold an agenda.

Key Question: Should the agendas of man hold more value than biblical principles? Why?

Key Terms: standing, right, scrutinized, disagreed, disregarded, forces, darkness

Key Take-Away for Today:

36. Allow negativity to hit you like water on top of goose feathers. Just allow it to roll right off.

Spiritual Content: Matthew 7:1-5
Judge not, that ye be not judged. For with what judgment ye judge, ye shall be judged: and with what measure ye mete, it shall be measured to you again. And why beholdest thou the mote that is in thy brother's eye, but considerest not the beam that is in thine own eye? Or how wilt thou say to thy brother, Let me pull out the mote out of thine eye; and, behold, a beam is in thine own eye? Thou hypocrite, first cast out the beam out of thine own eye; and then shalt thou see clearly to cast out the mote out of thy brother's eye.

Natural Content: Negativity will only take effect if you allow it to. Some individuals have a hard time working through their issues, so they amplify the issues of others to feel good about themselves.

Key Question: Why is it important to affirm positive thoughts about who you are?

Key Terms: negativity, goose feathers

Key Take-Away for Today:

37. We can become complacent to mediocrity or possess the drive to give real value to the world.

Spiritual Content: Ephesians 2:10
For we are his workmanship, created in Christ Jesus unto good works, which God hath before ordained that we should walk in them.

Natural Content: We were not created to be average but created in His image and likeness to have dominion. Therefore, if you want to know who you are, study who God is.

Key Question: What are some distractions that keep us from becoming the best version of ourselves?

Key Terms: become, complacent, mediocrity, possess, drive, value

Key Take-Away for Today:

38. You can always find the intent of a person based on time and loyalty.

Spiritual Content: Ruth 1:16-17
But Ruth replied, "Don't urge me to leave you or to turn back from you. Where you go I will go, and where you stay I will stay. Your people will be my people and your God my God. Where you die I will die, and there I will be buried. May the Lord deal with me, be it ever so severely, if even death separates you and me."

Natural Content: When evaluating the character of a person just be patient because life will bring its share of good days as well as bad. Time will always reveal who people truly are.

Key Question: What are some poor choices you have made without using patience?

Key Terms: find, truth, time, loyalty

Key Take-Away for Today:

39. The benefits of your mistakes ought to be wisdom. Otherwise, you will continue to look through the lens of a fool.

Spiritual Content: Proverbs 15:21-23
Foolishness brings joy to one without sense, but a man with understanding walks a straight path. Plans fail when there is no counsel, but with many advisers they succeed. A man takes joy in giving an answer; and a timely word—how good that is!

Natural Content: There will always be learning points in all that we do. A fool undermines correction because of pride. It is up to you as an individual to take heed and grow.

Key Question: Do you learn from your mistakes to never make them again?

Key Terms: benefits, mistakes, wisdom, otherwise, lens, fool

Key Take-Away for Today:

40. Disruption, division, and defeat began when there was a breakdown in communication that was never addressed.

Spiritual Content: 1 Corinthians 1:10-1310
Now I beseech you, brethren, by the name of our Lord Jesus Christ, that ye all speak the same thing, and that there be no divisions among you; but that ye be perfectly joined together in the same mind and in the same judgment. For it hath been declared unto me of you, my brethren, by them which are of the house of Chloe, that there are contentions among you. Now this I say, that every one of you saith, I am of Paul; and I of Apollos; and I of Cephas; and I of Christ. Is Christ divided? was Paul crucified for you? or were ye baptized in the name of Paul?

Natural Content: To stay on one accord, we must have an understanding by talking more constructively and feeling less offended.

Key Question: Why would your communication skills be offensive towards others?

Key Terms: disruption, division, defeat, breakdown, communication

Key Take-Away for Today:

41. Understand, not everyone wants to align with you nor should you align with everyone. But be mindful of who you align with because not everyone is in alignment.

Spiritual Content: 1 John 4:1
Beloved, believe not every spirit, but try the spirits whether they are of God: because many false prophets are gone out into the world.

Natural Content: What we want may not be God's plan for our lives. Seek his will and behold how opportunities present it-self before you.

Key Question: Are you seeking God to work his perfect will through you?

Key Terms: understand, align, everyone, mindful

Key Take-Away for Today:

42. It's about God's business. There is no other business. Cultivate the earth for His namesake and you shall be blessed.

Spiritual Content: Proverbs 20:24
A man's steps are directed by the Lord. How then can anyone understand his own way?

Natural Content: In all that, we do our works should bring glory to the kingdom of God. We are only required to be a vessel.

Key Question: What are you doing to advance the kingdom of heaven?

Key Terms: God, business, cultivate, earth, namesake, glory

Key Take-Away for Today:

43. Allow your vision to be without boundaries and, trust in the Lord from which all things originate.

Spiritual Content: Genesis 17:16
And I will bless her and give thee a son also of her: yea, I will bless her, and she shall be a mother of nations; kings of people shall be of her.

Natural Content: We serve a God who is limitless. Therefore, as children of The Highest what is it that we shall not have if we truly believe.

Key Question: When you pray do you believe wholeheartedly?

Key Terms: vision, boundaries, trust, Lord, originate

Key Take-Away for Today:

44. Remain humble because there is always room for self-improvement. A stubborn man will never be able to decipher constructive criticism.

Spiritual Content: 1 Peter 5:5
Likewise, ye younger, submit yourselves unto the elder. Yea, all [of you] be subject one to another and be clothed with humility: for God resisteth the proud, and giveth grace to the humble.

Natural Content: If you desire to grow as a person one must have humility. Recognize teachable moments and wisdom when it presents itself.

Key Question: Are you humble enough to accept your needs for self - improvement

Key Terms: remain, humble, self – improvement, stubborn, never, able, decipher, constructive, criticism

Key Take-Away for Today:

45. You must fix things internally before you can even attempt to have external value.

Spiritual Content: 1 Timothy 6:3-5
If any man teach otherwise, and consent not to wholesome words, even the words of our Lord Jesus Christ, and to the doctrine which is according to godliness; he is proud, knowing nothing, but doting about questions and strifes of words, whereof cometh envy, strife, railings, evil surmisings, perverse disputings of men of corrupt minds, and destitute of the truth, supposing that gain is godliness: from such withdraw thyself.

Natural Content: A warped mind has no value because it is incapable of producing truth. Therefore, whatever he or she releases to the world will cause more damage than good.

Key Question: Why is it important to purify ourselves before we pour into others?

Key Terms: fix, internally, attempt, external, value

Key Take-Away for Today:

46. You will have dilemmas in life, so why focus on matters that should be ignored? Use your time and energy wisely. Productivity is the most important.

Spiritual Content: James 1:2-4
Count it all joy, my brothers, when you meet trials of various kinds, for you know that the testing of your faith produces steadfastness. And let steadfastness have its full effect, that you may be perfect and complete, lacking in nothing.

Natural Content: We will all face bumps in the road, but God wants us to turn it all over to him and believe that he will work out the things that are within and beyond our control.

Key Question: What areas of your life are you wasting energy by focusing on the wrong things?

Key Terms: dilemmas, life, focus, ignored, time, energy, wisely, productivity, important

Key Take-Away for Today:

47. People do things according to their knowledge. If they knew better, they would do better.

Spiritual Content: Hosea 4:6
My people are destroyed for lack of knowledge: because thou hast rejected knowledge, I will also reject thee, that thou shalt be no priest to me: seeing thou hast forgotten the law of thy God, I will also forget thy children.

Natural Content: The level of significance your life can obtain is derived through the power of knowledge. Not only does knowledge have the ability to impact a greater existence for you but also for generations to come.

Key Question: How much of a hindrance are you to yourself by choosing not to seek knowledge?

Key Terms: according, knowledge, knew, better

Key Take-Away for Today:

48. Focus on the right thing instead of the left or right-wing.

Spiritual Content: Romans 12:2
And be not conformed to this world: but be ye transformed by the renewing of your mind, that ye may prove what is that good, and acceptable, and perfect, will of God.

Natural Content: Your political affiliation should not compromise your responsibility to humanity based on personal gain. You are an employee of the people by way of our labor and taxes.

Key Question: Are the needs of citizens being met in America?

Key Terms: focus, instead, left-wing, right-wing

Key Take-Away for Today:

49. Darkness begets darkness but the truth is the way and the light. The truth will always supersede darkness bringing forth the greater good.

Spiritual Content: 1 Peter 2:9
But ye [are] a chosen generation, a royal priesthood, a holy nation, a peculiar people; that ye should shew forth the praises of him who hath called you out of darkness into his marvelous light.

Natural Content: God wants to bring us out of darkness because within darkness is nothing but bondage. You will not experience what is good and abundant unless you come into light by way of truth.

Key Question: Why is the truth considered light?

Key Terms: darkness, begets, truth, way, light, supersede, greater – good

Key Take-Away for Today:

50. Money is synonymous with exposure and on the same hand, exposure is synonymous with money.

Spiritual Content: 1 Timothy 6:10
For the love of money is the root of all evil: which while some coveted after, they have erred from the faith, and pierced themselves through with many sorrows.

Natural Content: When you have money, you have the opportunity to see and experience much but, you will also see how money reveals and exposes individuals' behavior and character. In essence, one's characteristics will be amplified by money.

Key Question: What are some examples of how money has corrupted man?

Key Terms: money, synonymous, exposure

Key Take-Away for Today:

51. Stand clear of your association with those that utterly try to kill your will and assassinate your character. Their intentions will never be pure. They are controlled by an evil spirit.

Spiritual Content: Psalm 109:2-5
For wicked and deceitful mouths are opened against me, speaking against me with lying tongues. They encircle me with words of hate and attack me without cause. In return for my love they accuse me, but I give myself to prayer. So, they reward me evil for good, and hatred for my love.

Natural Content: Keep your eyes open and use discernment because not everyone you associate with has your best interest at heart. Give them little to no knowledge of you nor your personal life. It is better to cut them off and avoid them at all costs.

Key Question: Have you ever been around someone and your gut is signaling to you that something is off?

Key Terms: association, utterly, assassinate, character, intentions, pure, controlled, evil, spirit

Key Take-Away for Today:

52. Considering your doubts aspire to achieve and the atmosphere will shift in your favor. A marathon is impossible to complete with the intent of a sprint.

Spiritual Content: Jeremiah 29:11
For I know the thoughts that I think toward you, saith the LORD, thoughts of peace, and not of evil, to give you an expected end.

Natural Content: Take your time and believe in the process. Your breakthrough is coming. The blessing is always in your ability to endure.

Key Question: Do you tend to give up if you don't achieve your desired goal right away?

Key Terms: doubts, aspire, achieve, atmosphere, shift, favor, marathon, impossible, complete, sprint

Key Take-Away for Today:

53. Positive Thoughts Only!!!!!!! Affirm that you are in control of your emotions, views, and destiny.

Spiritual Content: Proverbs 17:22
A merry heart doeth good [like] a medicine: but a broken spirit drieth the bones.

Natural Content: Seek constructive conversations and environments because we become what we focus our attention on the most.

Key Question: How do you deal with negative energy and are you the source of it?

Key Terms: positive, thoughts, affirm, control, emotions, views, destiny

Key Take-Away for Today:

54. The word "can't" is a negative deterrent, and what we speak will surely be deposited into our spirit. I Can, I Must, I Will... are examples of words that produce life.

Spiritual Content: Proverb 18:21
Death and life [are] in the power of the tongue: and they that love it shall eat the fruit thereof.

Natural Content: "I will" continue to express how much control "I" have over "my" outcome based on the words "I" use to define "my" emotions, purpose, destination and being. "I think, therefore I am."

Key Question: Do you subconsciously curse yourself because of the words you speak?

Key Terms: can't, negative, deterrent, deposited, spirit, can, must, will, words, produce, life

Key Take-Away for Today:

55. Speak life and preserve the goodness of humanity it is the only way to balance an atmosphere consumed by darkness.

Spiritual Content: Ephesians 4:29
Let no unwholesome word proceed from your mouth, but only such a word as is good for edification according to the need of the moment, so that it will give grace to those who hear.

Natural Content: There is power in our words that build the strength of conviction necessary for our actions.

Key Question: Do you use dialogue to build others up or to tear people down?

Key Terms: speak, life, example, light

Key Take-Away for Today:

56. Not all dreams come true, but alternatives do. Continue to refine your natural ability, and success will find you.

Spiritual Content: Romans 8:18
For I consider that the sufferings of this present time are not worthy to be compared with the glory which shall be revealed in us.

Natural Content: Understand that your letdowns will be a set up for the great things that are to come. You cannot move about sporadically if you want to experience growth.

Key Question: Do you have a backup plan for your initial plan?

Key Terms: dreams, alternatives, continue, refine, natural, ability, success

Key Take-Away for Today:

57. Thoughts control our emotions.

Emotions control our actions.
Actions control our outcomes.

Spiritual Content: 2 Peter 1:5-7
For this very reason, make every effort to supplement your
faith with virtue, and virtue with
knowledge, and knowledge with self-control, and self-control
with steadfastness and
and steadfastness with godliness, and godliness with
brotherly affection, and brotherly
with love.

Natural Content: For all these things are intertwined around one common denominator, control.

Key Question: Do you take time to think before you act on situations?

Key Terms: thoughts, emotions, actions, outcomes, control

Key Take-Away for Today:

58. When you finally get tired of your shortcomings you will choose to do something about it. Though, the outcome could be extreme in either direction.

Spiritual Content: Matthew 6:33
But seek ye first the kingdom of God, and his righteousness; and all these things shall be added unto you.

Natural Content: The challenges of life will force your hand and at that moment you will be forced to make a good choice, (that of prosperity) or a bad choice, (that of damnation).

Key Question: What are you doing to prepare for your future?

Key Terms: finally, tired, shortcomings, choose, something

Key Take-Away for Today:

59. W.I.N

Why I Never - stop
Why I Never - quit
Why I Never - fail
WIN!

Spiritual Content: Philippians 3:12
Not that I have already obtained all this, or have already arrived at my goal, but I press on to take hold of that for which Christ Jesus took hold of me.

Natural Content: The enemy's mission is to prevent the initial intent of bringing the fullness of heaven to earth. We already have victory, but it is our responsibility to cultivate that victory in a natural state. Proceed to finish your race.

Key Question: What is your W.I.N, (why I never) ...?

Key Terms: win, why, I, never

Key Take-Away for Today:

60. When you're called to be the salt of the earth and the light of the world, good deeds are never a burden. Count it all joy. The authority of dominion is in knowing who you are.

Spiritual Content: Matthew 5:13-16
You are the salt of the earth. But if the salt loses its saltiness, how can it be made salty again? It is no longer good for anything, except to be thrown out and trampled underfoot. "You are the light of the world. A town built on a hill cannot be hidden. Neither do people light a lamp and put it under a bowl. Instead, they put it on its stand, and it gives light to everyone in the house. In the same way, let your light shine before others, that they may see your good deeds and glorify your Father in heaven.

Natural Content: It is an honor to serve as a Kingdom Citizen. Take pride in your ability, and with a joyful heart help others along the way. The greatest example of a selfless life is Jesus Christ.

Key Question: Are you an example that your community can be inspired by?

Key Terms: called, salt, earth, light, world, deeds, burden, joy

Key Take-Away for Today:

61. Have discipline or be disciplined.

Spiritual Content: Proverbs 13:18
Poverty and shame shall be to him that refuseth instruction: but he that regardeth reproof shall be honoured.

Natural Content: You will either have enough respect and control to abide or you will be dealt with accordingly. The entire universe operates by law.

Key Question: What areas of your life are you lacking discipline?

Key Terms: discipline, disciplined, obedience

Key Take-Away for Today:

62. Structure is essential and without the implementation of it the practice is lost; so too is respect. It will have no other choice other than to give way to confusion and chaos.

Spiritual Content: Romans 1:29-32
Being filled with all unrighteousness, fornication, wickedness, covetousness, maliciousness; full of envy, murder, debate, deceit, malignity; whisperers, backbiters, haters of God, despiteful, proud, boasters, inventors of evil things, disobedient to parents, Without understanding, covenant breakers, without natural affection, implacable, unmerciful: Who knowing the judgment of God, that they which commit such things are worthy of death, not only do the same, but have pleasure in them that do them.

Natural Content: As I witness these things come to pass in the generations of our youth. It reaffirms that socialist systems are in place to fulfill the agendas of population and mind control to hand over all authority established by wealth to the BEAST.

Key Question: Why is the appreciation of structure becoming offensive?

Key Terms: structure, essential, implementation, practice, lost, respect

Key Take-Away for Today:

63. Surely there is favor in obedience.

Spiritual Content: 1 Samuel 15:22
And Samuel said, Hath the Lord as great delight in burnt offerings and sacrifices, as in obeying the voice of the Lord? Behold, to obey is better than sacrifice, and to hearken than the fat of rams.

Natural Content: When you delight in something it means pleasure, adore, favor, honor, bless, protect, love... Quite naturally these are the things we want to be around and in our lives. Yet, the opposite of delight would be hatred, misery, sorrow, pain, depression, displeasure...

Key Question: What do you want for your life?

Key Terms: surely, favor, obedience

Key Take-Away for Today:

64. Operate in integrity, without ulterior motives and you shall be honored and exalted. God says He will pour out a blessing that you can't contain because He can trust you to do the right things with much.

Spiritual Content: 1 Kings 9:4-5
And if thou wilt walk before me, as David thy father walked, in integrity of heart, and in uprightness, to do according to all that I have commanded thee, and wilt keep my statutes and my judgments: Then I will establish the throne of thy kingdom upon Israel forever, as I promised to David thy father, saying, There shall not fail thee a man upon the throne of Israel.

Natural Content: There will always be honor in integrity. For integrity should be guarded like precious gold. You will be exalted amongst your enemies and positioned in authority without even seeking it.

Key Question: Do you make decisions based on motive?

Key Terms: operate, integrity, ulterior, motives, honored, exalted, blessing, contain, trust

Key Take-Away for Today:

65. If you dig deep enough you will get to the core of any source. Faint not, continue to push through circumstances that try to prevent you from the promises that are rightfully yours. All things of God are accessible if we believe and obey His laws, statutes, and commandments.

Spiritual Content: Galatians 6:7-9
Be not deceived; God is not mocked: for whatsoever a man soweth, that shall he also reap. For he that soweth to his flesh shall of the flesh reap corruption; but he that soweth to the Spirit shall of the Spirit reap life everlasting. And let us not be weary in well doing for in due season we shall reap, if we faint not

Natural Content: Often we are close to the finish line but are overwhelmed by frustration and throw in the towel. But if we learn to put our heads down and have some grit about ourselves there is nothing we can't obtain. As we obey the laws of God, we are set free from bondage.

Key Question: What laws have you broken that have caused your bondage?

Key Terms: core, source, faint, circumstances, prevent, promises, rightfully, accessible, believe, obey, laws, statutes, commandments

Key Take-Away for Today:

66. Study who God is so that you will know who you are, where you come from and why you are here.

Spiritual Content: 1 Corinthians 3:16
Know ye not that ye are the temple of God, and [that] the Spirit of God dwelleth in you?

Natural Content: The word human is derived by the root words humus (dirt) and man (spirit) which acknowledges God and you as a spirit. We are created in His image and likeness. Called out of darkness to be joint-heirs of the God Head. Your inheritance belongs to you because of your right of passage.

Key Question: Do you know who you are?

Key Terms: study, God

Key Take-Away for Today:

67. They say your reputation is like credit. I say charge it to the good and remain in good standing with others.

Spiritual Content: Proverbs 22:1
A good name is to be more desired than great wealth, Favor is better than silver and gold.

Natural Content: Do right by your name, and your name will always do right by you. Keys open doors. Secure the treasures that belong to you.

Key Question: Why would a reputation determine your success?

Key Terms: reputation, credit, charge, remain, standing

Key Take-Away for Today:

68. Nothing under the SUN/SON will ever be done in secret. God is omnipresent so He always knows the truth.

Spiritual Content: Ecclesiastes 12:14
For God shall bring every work into judgment, with every secret thing, whether [it be] good, or whether [it be] evil.

Natural Content: We know all things are possible but the ability to hide truth…, IMPOSSIBLE!

Key Question: Have you settled your secrets and differences with God and others?

Key Terms: sun, son, secret, God, omnipresent, truth

Key Take-Away for Today:

69. There are forces of darkness seen and unseen trying to destroy you every day. Reaffirm your position with the Lord by speaking his word and promises.

Spiritual Content: Psalms 23:1-6
The Lord is my shepherd; I shall not want. He maketh me to lie down in green pastures: he leadeth me beside the still waters. He restoreth my soul: he leadeth me in the paths of righteousness for his name's sake. Yea, though I walk through the valley of the shadow of death, I will fear no evil: for thou art with me; thy rod and thy staff they comfort me. Thou preparest a table before me in the presence of mine enemies: thou anointest my head with oil; my cup runneth over. Surely goodness and mercy shall follow me all the days of my life: and I will dwell in the house of the Lord forever.

Natural Content: To fight one must learn how to fight. The war on your life is in the spirit realm controlling our virtual reality.

Key Question: Do you know your family (generational) history?

Key Terms: forces, darkness, destroy, reaffirm, position, Lord, promises

Key Take-Away for Today:

70. You have been afforded rights not only on earth but also in heaven. Know your rights, dual citizen for they are the keys of the kingdom of heaven.

Spiritual Content: Matthew 16:19
I will give you the keys of the kingdom of heaven; whatever you bind on earth will be bound in heaven, and whatever you loose on earth will be loosed in heaven.

Natural Content: God's promises are true and through Him, they are done, but we will continue to have not if we ask not. You can unlock what is rightfully yours in heaven and it will be unlocked on earth. You also have the ability to lock up that which is in the earth and it will be locked up in the spirit. Victory is ours! Glory to God in the highest!!!

Key Question: What are the rights of a citizen that belongs to a kingdom?

Key Terms: afforded, earth, heaven, rights, dual, citizen, keys, kingdom

Key Take-Away for Today:

71. Love! And continue to love.

When you're hurt.
When you're betrayed.
When you're humiliated.
When you're broken.
Love!

Spiritual Content: 1 John 4:7-10
Dear friends, let us love one another, for love comes from God. Everyone who loves has been born of God and knows God. Whoever does not love does not know God, because God is love. This is how God showed his love among us: He sent his one and only Son into the world that we might live through him. This is love: not that we loved God, but that he loved us and sent his Son as an atoning sacrifice for our sins.

Natural Content: We live in a world of corruption, evil, hatred, and position of power by war. Love is and will always be the only answer for humanity. Love is the only force that will redeem the earth.

Key Question: What is love?

Key Terms: love, hurt, betrayed, humiliated, broken

Key Take-Away for Today:

72. Plant seeds of positivity because one simple gesture could be the seed that enabled someone to change the world.

Spiritual Content: Matthew 25:35-40
For I was hungry and you gave Me food; I was thirsty and you gave Me drink; I was a stranger and you took Me in; I was naked and you clothed Me; I was sick and you visited Me; I was in prison and you came to Me.' "Then the righteous will answer Him, saying, 'Lord, when did we see You hungry and feed You, or thirsty and give You drink? When did we see You a stranger and take You in, or naked and clothe You? Or when did we see You sick, or in prison, and come to You?' And the King will answer and say to them, 'Assuredly, I say to you, inasmuch as you did it to one of the least of these My brethren, you did it to Me.'

Natural Content: The heart of a servant will always manifest by one's actions. Not only is it an honor and privilege to be a blessing, but it is truly inspirational.

Key Question: How do your actions impact others?

Key Terms: plant, seeds, positivity, simple, gesture, enabled

Key Take-Away for Today:

73. There is no such thing as an overnight success. Your drive, your want, your hustle, and faith are the only way to become self - sufficient.

Spiritual Content: Proverbs 28:19-20
A hard worker has plenty of food, but a person who chases fantasies ends up in poverty. The trustworthy person will get a rich reward, but a person who wants quick riches will get into trouble.

Natural Content: After climbing the mountain you get to take in the view of beauty over the landscape. There is a greater appreciation of what you receive after the hard work you put in.

Key Question: What motivates you? What is your why?

Key Terms: success, drive, want, hustle, faith, self – sufficient

Key Take-Away for Today:

74. You have to establish an objective to have expectations. Otherwise, you will deal with assumptions that turn into an undesired outcome.

Spiritual Content: Genesis 9:11
And I will establish my covenant with you; neither shall all flesh be cut off any more by the waters of a flood; neither shall there any more be a flood to destroy the earth.

Natural Content: Some things have to take effect or put in place to have an understanding. When things are completely spelled out there should never be any misinterpretation.

Key Question: What are some undesired outcomes based on lack of communication?

Key Terms: establish, objective, order, expectations, otherwise, assumptions, undesired, outcome

Key Take-Away for Today:

75. In competition never assume that everyone is only putting in the work that is required of them. Those that want to be the best will always assess their situation and figure out an advantage.

Spiritual Content: 1 Corinthians 9:24
Do you not know that those who run in a race all run, but only one receives the prize? Run in such a way that you may win.

Natural Content: The greatest of winners win because they take what they are competing in seriously. They assess their situation to leverage improvement because the opportunity is constantly on their minds. They endure the grueling preparation phase because the gratification of achievement quenches the pain.

Key Question: What are you willing to endure to achieve your goals?

Key Terms: competition, assume, required, assess, situation, advantage

Key Take-Away for Today:

76. If you are naturally the best at your ability and or craft, do not become complacent. Recognize you have to work that much harder. For you are the motivation that others desire to be.

Spiritual Content: Proverbs 13:4
Lazy people want much but get little, but those who work hard will prosper.

Natural Content: If you combine work ethic with the gifted natural ability the combination will breed success causing competitors to always chase after you.

Key Question: Does your work ethic supersede your natural ability?

Key Terms: naturally, best, ability, craft, complacent, recognize, motivation, desire

Key Take-Away for Today:

77. There is no benefit to being spiteful. The truth is you will never win. But there is relief in forgiveness. It releases positive vibrations.

Spiritual Content: 2 Chronicles 7:14
If my people, which are called by my name, shall humble themselves, and pray, and seek my face, and turn from their wicked ways; then will I hear from heaven, and will forgive their sin, and will heal their land.

Natural Content: When we humble ourselves it softens the heart, drawing us closer to love and compassion. It creates a harmony of healing that we all need.

Key Question: Why would being spiteful result as a selfish act?

Key Terms: benefit, spiteful, truth, win, relief, forgiveness, releases, positive, vibrations

Key Take-Away for Today:

78. Everything is in a state of becoming. You either get better or worse. Nothing remains the same.

Spiritual Content: 2 Corinthians 5:17
Therefore if any man be in Christ, he is a new creation; old things have passed away, and look, new things have come.

Natural Content: Maximize your opportunities because just like life itself they too shall wither and die.

Key Question: What is your approach to growth? Is it necessary?

Key Terms: everything, state, becoming, better, worse, remains

Key Take-Away for Today:

79. The subconscious mind is nothing to play with. Guard your ear and eye gates to preserve #LIFEoverDEATH.

Spiritual Content: Ephesians 4:27
And give no opportunity to the devil.

Natural Content: The enemy is looking for any and every opportunity for your mind to be his playground. He wants to find a way to possess your mind because he ultimately wants to possess your soul.

Key Question: What gateways are you subject to allowing your mind to become possessed?

Key Terms: subconscious, mind, play, guard, gates, preserve

Key Take-Away for Today:

80. Hallelujah!

Spiritual Content: Psalm 148:1-2
Praise the Lord. Praise the Lord from the heavens; praise him in the heights above. Praise him all his angels; praise him, all his heavenly hosts.

Natural Content: Hallelujah, is a chant of yes! A coming in agreement with. Let us all shout hallelujah to the Most High for it is the highest praise.

Key Question: Are you conscience of having humility?

Key Terms: hallelujah

Key Take-Away for Today:

81. Everything begins in FAITH.

Spiritual Content: 1 Peter 1:6-9

In this you rejoice, though now for a little while, if necessary, you have been grieved by various trials, so that the tested genuineness of your faith—more precious than gold that perishes though it is tested by fire—may be found to result in praise and glory and honor at the revelation of Jesus Christ. Though you have not seen him, you love him. Though you do not now see him, you believe in him and rejoice with joy that is inexpressible and filled with glory, obtaining the outcome of your faith, the salvation of your souls.

Natural Content: You have to believe wholeheartedly to produce something out of nothing because in all things faith is the generator of manifestation.

Key Question: What do you see, and, are you willing to commit to what you see for yourself in the future?

Key Terms: everything, begins, faith

Key Take-Away for Today:

82. When you turn your desire into a sacrifice of pure intention you can attract. Fasting and prayer open the portal of communication to God with urgency.

Spiritual Content: 2 Corinthians 6:2
For he says, "In the time of my favor I heard you, and in the day of salvation I helped you." I tell you, now is the time of God's favor, now is the day of salvation.

Natural Content: Although God is omnipresent our willingness to sacrifice draws His attention more effectively. He will never leave thee nor forsake thee. He will always prove Himself faithful and show up in a mighty way.

Key Question: What type of results have fasting produced for you?

Key Terms: desire, sacrifice, pure, intention, ability, attract, fasting, prayer, portal, communication, God, urgency

Key Take-Away for Today:

83. Never count out a person that comes from a good foundation. No matter how much they mess up, they're bound to get it right.

Spiritual Content: Proverbs 22:6
Train up a child in the way he should go: and when he is old, he will not depart from it.

Natural Content: As we travel along the road of life, we may make a few wrong turns but like a navigation system our core principles and values will kick in and steer us the right way.

Key Question: What is the base of your foundation in the establishment of who you are?

Key Terms: never, good, foundation, bound, right

Key Take-Away for Today:

84. Pray with your family and children so they may agree with the covering or God's grace and mercy.

Spiritual Content: Joshua 24:15
But if serving the Lord seems undesirable to you, then choose for yourselves this day whom you will serve, whether the gods your ancestors served beyond the Euphrates, or the gods of the Amorites, in whose land you are living. But as for me and my household, we will serve the Lord."

Natural Content: A house that is divided shall not stand, and this is why God has to remain the focal point in all aspects of our living. Otherwise, we give way to the enemy becoming susceptible to his attacks on our lives.

Key Question: Are you renouncing the strongholds of division in your home?

Key Terms: pray, family, children, agreement, covering, God, grace, mercy

Key Take-Away for Today:

85. All energy is attached to a spirit. Never profess something nor claim to belong to something you do not know of. Your due diligence is the only way to the truth. We open ourselves up to blessings or curses by the covenants we make.

Spiritual Content: 2 Timothy 2:15
Study to shew thyself approved unto God, a workman that needeth not to be ashamed, rightly dividing the word of truth.

Natural Content: Never come into anything without having full knowledge of its history and truth. The more knowledge you have the harder it is to be misled.

Key Question: What are you studying to become aware of the vices and traps of the enemy?

Key Terms: energy, attached, spirit, profess, claim, belong, knowledge, diligence, truth, open, blessings, curses, covenants

Key Take-Away for Today:

86. When your spirit is in the right place so too shall be your actions and soul.

Spiritual Content: Luke 10:27
And he answering said, Thou shalt love the Lord thy God with all thy heart, and with all thy soul, and with all thy strength, and with all thy mind; and thy neighbour as thyself.

Natural Content: These elements will always be in conjunction with one another, therefore, be filled with the holy spirit to be influenced by righteous conviction.

Key Question: What type of spirit are your actions influenced by?

Key Terms: spirit, right, soul, actions

Key Take-Away for Today:

87. Never allow your craft or your talents to define you. It is a mere portion of who you are. Your impact on the world will be through the gift of the Father. Man-made legacies will never last for eternity.

Spiritual Content: Matthew 24:33-35
So you also, when you see all these things, know that [a]it is near—at the doors! Assuredly, I say to you, this generation will by no means pass away till all these things take place. Heaven and earth will pass away, but My words will by no means pass away.

Natural Content: Never deceive yourself into believing because you have multiple abilities you are guaranteed success. Our responsibility is to share our ordained gift to cultivate and make a difference in the lives of others.

Key Question: Are you seeking the Father by way of the holy spirit to find the gift/calling on your life?

Key Terms: never, allow, craft, talents, define, mere, portion, impact, gift, Father, man, made, legacies, eternity

Key Take-Away for Today:

88. GOD LIVES EVERYWHERE AROUND ME
(G.L.E.A.M)

Spiritual Content: Colossians 1:16
For by him were all things created, that are in heaven, and that are in earth, visible and invisible, whether [they be] thrones, or dominions, or principalities, or powers: all things were created by him, and for him: And he is before all things, and by him all things consist.

Natural Content: God is and will forever be omnipresent. He is the G.L.E.A.M of my life and this world.

GLEAM – (of an emotion or quality) appear or be expressed through the brightness of someone's eyes or expression.

Key Question: When will you commit to God being omnipresent in your life?

Key Terms: god, lives, everywhere, around, me

Key Take-Away for Today:

www.ingramcontent.com/pod-product-compliance
Lightning Source LLC
Chambersburg PA
CBHW032058150426
43194CB00006B/574